LAND AND WATER

Please visit our web site at: **www.garethstevens.com**
For a free color catalog describing our list of high-quality books,
call 1-800-542-2595 (USA) or 1-800-387-3178 (Canada).

Library of Congress Cataloging-in-Publication Data

Flow.
    Land and water.
        p. cm. — (Discovery Channel school science: our planet Earth)
    Originally published: Flow. Bethesda, Md.: Discovery Enterprises. © 2000.
    Summary: Explores the origins and effects of water on the landscape
including the formation of caves and deserts.
    ISBN-13: 978-0-8368-3381-2 (lib. bdg.)
    ISBN-10: 0-8368-3381-3 (lib. bdg.)
    1. Water—Juvenile literature. 2. Landforms—Juvenile literature.
[1. Water. 2. Landforms.] I. Title. II. Series.
GB662.3.F63 2004
551.48—dc22   2003059206

This edition first published in 2004 by
Gareth Stevens Publishing
A Weekly Reader® Company
1 Reader's Digest Road
Pleasantville, NY 10570-7000 USA

Further resources for students and educators available at
www.discoveryschool.com

Designed by Bill SMITH STUDIO
Creative Director: Ron Leighton
Designers: Sonia Gauba, Eric Hoffsten, Dmitri Kushnirsky, Bill Wilson,
    Jay Jaffe
Photo Editors: Jennifer Friel, Scott Haag
Intern: Chris Pascarella
Art Buyers: Paula Radding, Rae Grant

Gareth Stevens Editor: Betsy Rasmussen
Gareth Stevens Art Director: Tammy West
Technical Advisor: Sara Bruening

Printed in the United States of America

2 3 4 5 6 7 8 9 10 09 08 07

Writers: Michael Burgan, Judy Gitenstein, Kenn Goin, Donna O'Meara, Monique
Peterson, Gary Raham, Dennis Shealy, Alicia Slimmer, Lisa Trumbauer.

Editor: Kenn Goin

Photographs: pp. 2 & 5, people in boat, © Michael O'Leary/
DCI; p. 3 & 22–23, water drop; © PhotoDisc; p. 4, cattle,
Bettmann/CORBIS; p. 5, family in Amarillo, TX, © CORBIS;
pp. 4–5 & 13, Dust Bowl town, © CORBIS; pp. 6 & 9, river,
© Will & Deni McIntyre/Stone; p. 8, valley, © Jim Steinberg,
delta, © Color-Pic/NASA; p. 9, Bonneville Salt Flats, © Dean
Conger/Corbis; mudflow, © Roger Ressmeyer/ CORBIS; p. 12,
H. Bennett, Courtesy of the USDA, Natural Resources

Conservation Service; p. 13, Dust Bowl w/cowboy, © Bettmann/ CORBIS; p. 15,
Mark Twain, © Brown Brothers, Ltd.; p. 17, © Paul Sowder/DCI; pp. 18–19,
    Johnstown Flood (all), © Brown Brothers, Ltd.; p.24–25, all
    courtesy Karl Pohlmann; p. 30, microorganisms, © US Dept of
    the Interior/National Parks Service; p. 31, sinkhole, US Dept of
    the Interior/National Parks Service; Cover and all other photos,
    © Corel. **Illustration:** p. 20, formation of soil, Joe Veno.

Illustrations: p. 20, formation of soil, Joe Veno

Acknowledgments: pp. 18–19, excerpts from JOHNSTOWN:
THE DAY THE DAM BROKE by Richard O'Connor. © 1957,
J. B. Lippincott Company.

Discovery CHANNEL SCHOOL SCIENCE

CONTENTS

LAND AND WATER

Water has shaped and carved our planet throughout its history. Rivers have sculpted canyons and built deltas. Water does its work underground, as well. Secret streams have hollowed out caves and crevices and sometimes caused ground surfaces to collapse.

The ground may look solid and still, but the forces of water and wind are changing it bit by bit every day. In LAND and WATER, Discovery Channel shows you more about the fascinating (and often surprising) interactions between land and water.

Land & Water 4
At-a-Glance Find out how land and water work together, and what can go wrong when other forces upset the balance.

Watch Your Mouth. 6
Q & A A river goes pretty much where it wants. And along the way, it can really rearrange things.

Land Shaper 8
Picture This Canyons, glaciers, lakes, and mudflows—how water has ruled the land.

Water World 10
Timeline Conserving water is an idea that's been around ever since people started farming thousands of years ago.

Black Sky 12
Heroes Hugh Hammond Bennett put it all together to reverse the Dust Bowl disaster. Good land management requires good water management —and vice versa.

Old Man River 14
Almanac All about the heart, soul, and body of the United States' premier river—the Mississippi.

In the Flood Zone....................... 16
Map Floods can occur near any river, but some rivers make life a lot harder for people.

Where does water go? See page 22.

Soaked 18
Eyewitness Account What was the worst flood in U.S. history like? How did people recover from it? Read these accounts of the destruction and rebuilding of Johnstown, Pennsylvania.

Diggin' Up the Dirt 20
Scrapbook All about nature's recipe for soil—just mix rocks, wind, water, and plants and simmer for five hundred years.

Water-Drop Odyssey 22
Virtual Voyage Live life as a water molecule and travel through the water cycle for several millennia.

Seeking the Source 24
Scientist's Notebook Not much water in the desert, is there? There's more water there than you'd think. Finding it is the challenge. Where does the water come from? One scientist's quest.

Earth's Cellar 26
Amazing but True Water carves magnificent caves and creates splendid underground designs.

Trouble at Red Rock Ranch . . 28
Solve-It-Yourself Mystery One of these ranchers has a lot of explaining to do . . . and it's all about dirt on some boots!

Waterlogged 30
Fun & Fantastic A special table, natural fountains, quizzes, and stupendous little droplets about water.

Final Project

Lifeline. 32
Your World, Your Turn Water always flows from your taps. Your community stays safe from dangerous floods. Learn more about what keeps your water running and the land around you safe to live in.

3

Land & Water

The Great Plains, April 14, 1935

The first sound was the birds. Hundreds of them flitted nervously on the ground. Thousands more flew through the air, a mass of black against the darkening sky. The birds knew before the people did: Something terrible was about to happen.

The temperature hovered near 90°F (32°C) that Sunday afternoon. The Sun baked the dry farmlands of the Great Plains. Then the warm air turned unusually cool, and the wind began to howl. A massive cloud of thick, black dust rolled over the Plains.

Reaching more than 1 mile (2 kilometer) high, the dust storm turned day into night. Headlights were useless against the cloud, and cars crashed as the dust swirled around them. "It just roared right in," said Art Leonard, of Dodge City, Kansas. "I thought the end of the world was here." People groped on their hands and knees to reach their homes.

This dust storm was the worst one ever to hit the Great Plains, and the day is still remembered as "Black Sunday." A particularly parched area of Texas, Oklahoma, Kansas, Colorado, and New Mexico soon had a new nickname: the Dust Bowl.

What Happened?

Too little rain during the 1930s left the soil dry and powdery. The native prairie grasses, with long roots for finding water deep below the ground's surface, had been stripped away as farmers planted wheat and other crops. Without enough rain to moisten the topsoil or the deep root systems to hold it in place, the fine dirt was carried away by the wind. Only heavy rains could end this drought, and they finally arrived in 1939.

Downpours after a long dry spell bring sweet relief from heat and dust, but they can also bring more problems—major problems like flooding. Heavy rain falling fast runs off the land instead of sinking in. Without plants and their root systems to soak up and hold water, the problem becomes worse. Water runs off even faster, eroding the soil and causing rivers to fill up and spill over into the floodplain.

Land and water are two colossal forces locked together with an unbreakable bond. Water shapes land the way a sculptor shapes clay. But where water goes and what happens to it depend on the condition of the land under it. To understand how Earth works, you can't think of one without the other.

Cattle starved from lack of vegetation in the Dust Bowl.

About Drought

Periods of drought alternating with periods of plentiful precipitation are common in many parts of the world. Although rainfall was above average in most of the United States in the twentieth century, more than half of the country experienced drought in the 1930s.

A family of tenant farmers in Amarillo, Texas, was impoverished by drought.

Two people paddle down a street flooded by heavy rains.

SPEED LIMIT 35

WATCH YOUR MOUTH

THE LIFE AND TIMES OF A RIVER

Q: **You're a river. We hear you have lots of stories to tell.**

A: Well, you know rivers—we all have pretty big mouths. But I guess my life has been pretty interesting. Unpredictable. Never know what's around the next bend.

Q: **Why don't you tell us how it all began?**

A: OK. It's basically the same story for all rivers. It often starts with rain. Rain falls. More rain falls, then more and more.

Q: **And the rain pools on the ground and starts flowing? End of story?**

A: Nope, just the beginning. Some rain soaks into the ground. Some evaporates into the air. Still

more is taken up by plants and then evaporates out of their leaves. Finally, the water left on top starts flowing over the land, forming skinny little streams that tumble and babble over rocks and crannies. Those are the headwaters. Before long, those streams find a path downhill.

Q: **Why do they move downhill? Why not just stay put?**

A: For the same reason everything on Earth is pulled downward. A force called gravity drags the water downhill, and eventually these little streams run together to form a trunk: a wide, powerful river like me, ready to pick up my load and carry it to the end of the line—to some big body of water like a bay or a huge lake or the ocean.

Q: **I beg your pardon—your load?**

A: Sure. Moving water never travels empty-handed. Every brook, creek, and stream sweeps up and carries along tons of materials—that's the load.

Q: What kinds of materials?

A: All kinds. Anything we happen to run into; we're not fussy. Debris. Boulders. Twigs and leaves. Soil. Insects and other living things. Tiny grains of gravel and sand. Microscopic specks of minerals washed out of rocks and soil. You name it, some river has probably swept it away.

Q: How do rivers move all that stuff?

A: When it comes to transporting things, rivers have all the right moves. Big boulders are bounced and rolled along the bottom, or the bed. Twigs, branches, and leaves float on the surface. Minerals dissolve in the water, so they're invisible. But sand and soil stay suspended, at least when the flow is fast. That's why many rivers look especially brownish and muddy—they're carrying a lot of sediment.

Q: What happens to the sediment?

A: Sometimes it's deposited along the river's edge, where the water is shallow and friction with the riverbanks and bed slows things down naturally. The deeper water in the middle moves faster. It makes all kinds of neat whirlpools and eddies that go every which way and keep some of the load moving along.

Q: What's the point of making all these deposits of sediment and stuff?

A: What, you never heard of a riverbank? Just kidding. The point of all this dropping stuff off is to create new landscapes and landforms. See, rivers are builders. That's our job, and we do it well. Every time we unload, the landscape changes.

Q: That sounds very constructive and helpful.

A: Well, not always, I gotta be honest. Sometimes we're destructive. Rivers destroy as much as they build. Just can't help it. It's all about power. Flowing water is one of the most powerful forces on Earth. It has lots of energy, both to move things and to erode them. It can even cut through solid rock, if you give it enough time. Rivers chip away at huge boulders in their paths, until after awhile they're reduced to big stones, ready to be tumbled down the course. We make cuts and slices in our own banks. When we overflow, we can chew big bites out of paved roads. And when we're carrying a load of rough, edgy rocks, our job is even easier. Those make great cutting tools.

Q: But what about during a drought, when no rain falls for days, weeks—or sometimes months? Doesn't all your power disappear, along with all your water?

A: Nope. Luckily, rivers don't have to depend directly on rainfall for all their water. Some of it comes from underground, where it's stored in springs. In fact, some rivers get as much as half of their water supply from underground.

Q: Since you're always making deposits, how much of your load is left by the time you get to your mouth?

A: It depends on the course of the river, what the bed's made of, the way it flows—lots of things. But some rivers dump out so much sediment at the mouth that they create deltas—fan-shaped islands sometimes big enough to hold whole cities. New Orleans, Louisiana, is built on the Mississippi River's delta. Sediment makes nice, rich soil—full of minerals and great for farming.

Q: One last question: Do you ever get tired of running and just want to stop?

A: No way. Rivers have rich, full, long lives. Every stage lets us make a different kind of mark on the land. Young rivers begin to gouge out steep canyons. Older rivers flow through channels widened by erosion. There's never a dull moment, and if we do feel tired, we can always slow down and meander. That's when we form lazy, swoopy, snakelike curves. Very relaxing. You ought to try it.

Q: Well, I'll keep it in mind. Meanwhile, thanks for talking with us.

A: Sure. What else are mouths for? So long—and go with the flow.

Activity

KNOW YOUR RIVER! Find a map of your state or region. Is there a river that begins and ends within your area? Use one marker color to highlight the river and another color to highlight tributaries. Circle the river's source. Is there a delta? Circle it as well.

Research industries along the river. Mark each one on the map. Also mark major landmarks near the river, such as mountains, canyons, and lakes.

Land Shaper

I t's no contest. When water and land go head-to-head, the water wins. The power of flowing water and ice has helped shape Earth's surface for billions of years. Here is some of the work water has done—and continues doing every day.

Rolling Along

W hether it's a tiny brook or a mighty river, flowing freshwater is called a stream. The movement of streams is one of the most powerful land shapers on Earth. As a stream rolls along, it erodes the land beneath it, taking away sediment—bits of rock, sand, and minerals.

When a stream erodes hard rock, it carves out sediment and forms steep walls called canyons. The rushing waters of the Snake River carved Hell's Canyon on the border of Idaho and Oregon.

As a stream comes to flat ground or plains, it cuts curves through the landscape. These curves are called meanders, and their location changes over time. The sediment from one part of a curve gradually moves downstream and forms the beginning of a new curve. A stream repeats this process over time, so the meanders are always moving farther downstream.

Larger streams—called rivers—sometimes end in a delta, a point where flowing water meets a lake or sea. When conditions are just right—when waves in the large body of water are not too strong—sediment collects at the meeting point, creating islands. The fourth largest delta in the world is at the mouth of the Mississippi River.

The Snake River carved out Hell's Canyon.

Mississippi Delta

Glacier National Park

Cold Creator

You might consider ice as frozen in place, but some kinds of ice really know how to move. Glaciers are huge "rivers of ice" that cross mountains and land. During the Great Ice Age, about ten thousand years ago, sheets of glacial ice thousands of feet (meters) thick covered one-third of Earth. As they moved, these glaciers eroded the mountain valleys around them. The glaciers also carried some of the eroded rocks to new locations, just as rivers carry sediment. Glacial activity shaped many of the valleys in Glacier National Park in Montana (above).

'Round the Bend

The shaping power of streams and glaciers helped form many of the world's lakes. A meandering stream can create sharp S-shaped bends. Over time, the stream may cut a new channel through land to connect these bends. The old meanders are left behind, forming crescent-shaped pools of water known as oxbow lakes. More spectacular are the lakes created by glaciers, called ice-scour lakes. The Great Lakes, in the northern United States, were formed when glaciers carved hollow spots in the land. Melting ice and other freshwater then filled the hollows.

Lakes may seem to be unchanging, but water flows in and out of them all the time. A particular water molecule may remain in a lake for days or for hundreds of years. But if new water doesn't come in, the lake will disappear. Utah's vast Great Salt Lake Desert was once covered by Lake Bonneville. The water in the lake evaporated over time. Eventually, parts of the lake dried up, creating the Bonneville Salt Flat (below).

Oxbow lake

Bonneville Salt Flat

Muddy Mess

When soil, water, and gravity meet, mudflows result. These slides occur when heavy rains mix with loose soil or rocks on sloping land. Gravity is always acting on a slope to pull down loose soil and rocks—this is called soil creep. Water, added to the gravity, creates a river of moving mud. The mudflow changes the terrain by carrying soil down the slope and distributing it on the flat land below. Volcanic eruptions also create mudflows, as volcanic ash mixes with rain or melted snow. These are called lahars, and they frequently cause more deaths than the eruptions. Huge lahars followed the 1980 eruption of Mount St. Helens in Washington. Mudflows can travel up to 40 miles (64 km) per hour, carrying along cars, trees, and other objects in their path.

When Mount Unzen erupted in 1990, a mudflow destroyed many homes in Japan.

Activity

MINIATURE COMPRESSOR The force of gravity causes river water to flow, but it's the pressure of the water that shapes the land. To see the effects of pressure, try this experiment.

Materials

- 2 plastic bowls, each half-filled with sand
- measuring cup

Step 1. Hold one cup of water 6 inches (15 centimeters) above one bowl. Pour the contents evenly over the surface of the sand until the cup is empty.

Step 2. Repeat step 1 with the second bowl, but pour the water over the same place in the sand.

Describe how a concentrated flow of water affects the sand.

Water World

In ancient times when farmers dug canals to bring water to crops, they were performing the first experiments in hydrology—the science of how water gets from one place to another, and what happens to it along the way. Modern hydrologists study the water cycle and bodies of water, develop new soil conservation and farming techniques, design projects that help control flooding and drought, and improve how we use our natural resources. Follow the timeline to see how we got to where we are now: A world in which 25 percent of the electricity generated is water powered.

5000–2900 B.C.

In ancient Egypt, farmers take advantage of the annual flooding of the usually dry land of the Nile riverbank by planting crops to coincide with the rising water. They construct channels to carry water to the farmland and are able to contain the water so it can be used later as needed. In 2900 B.C., King Menes builds a dam —a barrier built across a body of water to control the flow—on the Nile to supply the Egyptian city of Memphis with water.

290–212 B.C.

Greek philosopher Archimedes invents a water pump in which water moves up the tube when a screw is turned. Originally invented to pump water from leaking ships, this pump is also used to pump water from wells to irrigate crops. Pumps based on Archimedes's idea are still used for pumping sewage in water treatment plants.

1000s

European farmers experiment with crop rotation, planting a summer crop in one section of a field and a winter crop in another. Nothing is planted on the third section to give the soil a rest. This keeps the field fertile for future crops. It also prevents farmers from having to move their farmland to another area when the soil wears out.

1600s

Frenchman Pierre Perrault proves that rain, snow, and sleet can account for all the water in a river. This disproves the long-standing idea that most of the water in streams and rivers comes from underground sources. Around this time, Englishman Edmond Halley collects data on wind, precipitation, and other meteorological phenomena. Perrault and Halley's research lays the groundwork for the study of hydrology as a science.

In Egypt, farmers constructed channels to carry water to their farmland.

An Egyptian farmer pumps water from a canal with an Archimedes screw.

Itaipú Dam

Mid-1800s

Scottish civil engineer William J. M. Rankine's work in the field of soil mechanics leads to new concepts in dam design. New dams are being built taller and wider. France's Furens Dam, completed in 1866, is considered to be the first dam of this type.

1930s

The United States begins work on large-scale hydrological projects. These water management systems provide controlled water movement and flood control, reservoirs, hydroelectric power, and bodies of water for recreational use over much of the country. One such system includes the Hoover Dam on the Colorado River, which controls water in California and Mexico. Engineers realize that the dam's construction calls for thick layers of concrete that would take more than one hundred years to cool and solidify. They decide to pump cold water through pipes already laid in place and then fill these pipes with concrete. The cold water allows the concrete to dry much quicker—and in one piece.

1991 and Beyond

The Itaipú Dam is completed on the Parana River between Brazil and Paraguay in South America. It is the largest hydroelectric dam in the world, stretching more than 5 miles (8 km) and containing eighteen gigantic turbines—machines that use a series of buckets, paddles, or blades. The amount of iron and steel used to create it could build 380 Eiffel Towers! Plus, it creates enough power to charge up most of California. Yet when completed, China's Three Gorges Dam on the Yangtze River and Turkey's Ataturk Dam will be even bigger.

HOOVER DAM

Activity

WHAT A DRIP! People place great value on conserving water. See for yourself how every drop counts! Turn a faucet so that it drips slightly, and place a measuring cup under the drip for fifteen minutes. (Be sure to turn the tap off after the time has passed.) Note the amount of water that dripped into the cup. Multiply that amount by 4 to see how much water will be wasted in an hour. Then multiply that result by 24 to see how much water will be lost in a day. Now imagine thousands and thousands of homes with leaky faucets—that's a lot of water down the drain!

Black Sky

Hugh Hammond Bennett (below) stood before Congress, urging its members to fund the Soil Conservation Act. It would make soil and water conservation a national priority in the United States. Suddenly, he threw back the curtains in the hearing room to reveal a sky black with dust from the Great Plains. The dust had been blown thousands of miles by the wind. The city of Washington was, for the first time, feeling the suffocating grime of the prairie's topsoil in its air. The dirt had even sifted through cracks in windows and landed on the desk of President Franklin D. Roosevelt.

Congress quickly allocated the money. It was one of many triumphs for Bennett, the first chief of the U.S. Soil Conservation Service.

Ecological Disaster

As a young man, Hugh Hammond Bennett worked as a surveyor for the Bureau of Soils. There he saw firsthand how certain kinds of farming could lead to crop failure.

By the time he took his post as Soil Conservation Chief in 1934, Bennett had developed strong opinions of what constituted good agricultural practices. And President Franklin Delano Roosevelt was firmly behind him. Both men knew that radical action was imperative to reverse the ravages of the Dust Bowl, the ecological disaster that haunted the United States throughout the 1930s.

At first, Bennett's ideas weren't popular. His insistence that some lands be left untilled each year meant less revenue for farmers. He had also said, "Americans have been the greatest destroyers of land of any race or people, barbaric or civilized." The farmers felt Bennett was saying they didn't know how to do their job.

Yet Bennett knew that any wide-scale conservation effort in the United States needed the backing of private landowners, especially farmers, who owned three-quarters of all land in the country. So he worked tirelessly to gain their support by helping them see the land and its problems in a new way.

The Soil

In the early part of the twentieth century, the study of soil was new. Yet the amount of land farmed in the United States was increasing dramatically. Vast areas of the Great Plains were being stripped of native vegetation and replanted with crops. Such practices didn't take into account either the propensity toward drought in the region or the topsoil's fragility. Bennett estimated that massive amounts of farm and grazing land were destroyed or in jeopardy.

What could he do? Bennett called attention to his cause through hundreds of rousing speeches and publications. He also took a number of other important steps.

First, he assembled a team of experts to try

to solve the problems of conserving native soils. Second, he called for each farm to be treated as an ecologically unique entity that required specifically tailored farming, grazing, and water resource strategies. "Put every acre to its best use and treat every acre according to its needs," he stated. Third, he ordered that small farming projects be set up to try new conservation techniques. The projects that succeeded could be used throughout the nation.

Lastly, Bennett made sure that farmers understood that all of these efforts would benefit them as well as the nation. For example, if one of his teams found a farm with worn-out soils, they helped the farmer find other uses for the land, such as for wildlife habitats or growing productive orchards. In many cases, farmers were even paid to *not* plant.

Drought and erosion devastated farming communities all across the Midwest in the 1930s.

The Water

Land, Bennett realized, was only half the problem. The other half was water. "Unrestrained erosion cannot but contribute to the hazards of floods," he said in 1936. Indeed, only seven years earlier, the Mississippi had risen "out of its banks in the wildest rampage" on record.

Until the 1930s, the government engineers dealt with flooding by building various structures in an attempt to control rivers. Bennett realized that this strategy didn't take into account the source of the problem—the loss of topsoil that let water simply run off the land rather than trapping it:

When a pitcher of water is spilled on the surface of a tilted wooden table, the water rushes off immediately and forms a puddle on the floor. But what happens when the hard wooden table is covered with a blotter and then a heavy Turkish towel? Most of the water is absorbed. . . . The same principle applies to the land. When it is bare, the raindrops falling on it rush off into the nearest stream or river. . . . When the land is covered with rich absorptive topsoil, made porous by the

hidden conduits of burrowing earthworms, insects and the roots of plants, as well as the natural granularity of such soil, you have a blotter for rain. And vegetation . . . forms countless tiny impediments to the downhill flow of any excess rainwater which the soil is unable to absorb.

Bennett improved the water management system by using a multiresource team approach, rather than relying solely on engineers. This method of flood control prevented many future disasters and saved millions of dollars.

By the time he retired in 1951, Bennett had changed land and water use in the United States forever. His agency, now called the Natural Resources Conservation Service, continues to work to keep America's landscape healthy and green.

Activity

SEE FOR YOURSELF Try this erosion-analogy experiment. You need two cups of water.
- Pour one cup of water on concrete or asphalt. Describe what happens.
- Pour the second cup of water on a plot of grass. Describe what happens.
- Describe how pouring water on concrete produces the same result as pouring water on badly eroded land.

Old Man River

GREAT RIVER ROAD

U.S. POSTAGE 5c

Without the Nile, Egypt would be all desert. Without the Amazon, countless species of plants and animals in the rain forest would be homeless—and maybe gone forever. And without the Mississippi, North America would be missing its center—and the United States would be missing a big part of its heartland. All rivers have an impact on their surroundings, but these large rivers affect huge regions and even entire countries.

Measuring the Mississippi

Length	2,348 miles (3,778 km)—The entire length of the country from Minnesota to the Gulf of Mexico
Width at widest point (north of St. Louis, Missouri)	7,000 feet (2,134 m)—About 1.5 miles (2.4 km)
Width at narrowest point (near Lake Itasca, Minnesota)	12 feet (3.7 m)—About the length of a minivan
Rate of flow	Average of 2 mph (3.2 kph)—Like a very slow walk
Rate of discharge into the Gulf of Mexico	600,000 cubic feet (16,890 cubic meters) per second
Typical winter depth (New Orleans)	30 feet (9 m)
Typical spring depth (New Orleans)	62 feet (19 m)
Number of states bordered	10
Number of tributaries	250
Number of fish species	240

Heart of the Heartland

A river is more than a waterway. The land around the river, called its watershed or basin, shares a river's ecological life. It can be drastically affected by changes in a river's condition, such as flooding or pollution. The Mississippi River basin is enormous, covering more than 1,200,000 square miles (3,108,000 sq km), or about one-eighth of the North American continent.

Drainage basin of the Mississippi River and its major tributaries.

STACK 'EM UP

Here is how other North American rivers measure up to the Mississippi.

Miles	0	500	1000	1500	2000	2500	3000	3500	4000

Mississippi	2,348 miles (3,778 km)
Missouri	2,315 miles (3,725 km)*
Yukon	1,979 miles (3,184 km)
Rio Grande	1,900 miles (3,057 km)
Arkansas	1,459 miles (2,348 km)*
Colorado	1,450 miles (2,333 km)
Red	1,290 miles (2,076 km)
Columbia	1,243 miles (2,000 km)
Snake	1,038 miles (1,670 km)
Ohio	981 miles (1,578 km)*

The Mississippi is the fifteenth longest river in the world. The top three:

Nile	4,160 miles (6,693 km)
Yangtze	3,964 miles (6,378 km)
Amazon	3,912 miles (6,294 km)

*Mississippi tributary

Control Yourself

Every spring, heavy rainfall and melting snow cause the Mississippi's waters to rise. As a result, major flood-control structures have been built by the U.S. Army Corps of Engineers to regulate the rate of water flow and to keep the waters back. At the mouth of the river, a network of channels, including spillways, cutoffs, and floodways, guide water safely to the gulf.

Number of locks and dams	29
Combined length of flood walls, dikes, levees (from Cairo, Illinois, south)	Over 2,000 miles (3,218 km)
Average height of levee	21 feet (6.4 m)

Locks raise and lower boats as they pass through different water levels on the river.

Mark My Words

The Mississippi River is mighty famous in literature, thanks to Mark Twain (right), author of the books *The Adventures of Tom Sawyer* and *Life on the Mississippi*. Twain once worked as a steamboat captain on the river, which he described as a "wonderful book, [with] a new story every day." His real name was Samuel Clemens, but he chose "Mark Twain" as a pen name because it refers to an old expression to describe the river's depth.

Twain was not the first person to describe the river. The Ojibwa Indians of Wisconsin called it "Missi Sipi," which means "Big River." The Algonquian Indians, who lived along the often-flooded lower valley, called it "father of waters." In folklore and songs the river is called the Mighty Mississippi, Big Muddy, Old Devil River, and Old Man River.

Activity

DON'T HAVE TO BE LONG TO BE FAMOUS
Even short rivers have played major roles in American history. Choose any American river (the James, Potomac, St. Lawrence, or Tallahatchie, for example). Highlight it on a map. Use note cards to identify locations along the river where historical events occurred. Get to know your river. Find out its special character—the animals that live in or near it, its width, its clarity, and so on. Attach your list to the bottom of your map.

What a Dump!

What has four mouths and spits sediments into the sea? The Mississippi Delta. That is where the Mississippi River dumps 220 million tons (200 million tonnes) of sediment into the Gulf of Mexico annually. The sediment is rich in minerals, though, so the surrounding area is fertile farmland. And it's a lot of land: The delta covers 10,100 square miles (26,159 sq km), an area about twice the size of the state of Connecticut. And the four mouths? Four separate channels of the river meet and greet at the delta.

15

In the Flood Zone

NORTH AMERICA

UNITED STATES

Paddle boat on the Mississippi

The Mississippi–Missouri–Ohio River System ①

VENEZUELA

The Orinoco River ②

The Amazon River System ③

BRAZIL

SOUTH AMERICA

All rivers flood—it's a fact of nature. Although floods can be destructive to human settlements, they can also be a great resource. Each time a stream overruns its banks, it brings rich sediment to the land, creating fertile soil for raising crops.

Most floods give some advance warning as they slowly develop. But sometimes flash floods catch people and wildlife off guard, with devastating results. This map shows the major rivers of the world and areas rich in fertile land where people have had to grapple with the high risks of floods.

① The Mississippi–Missouri–Ohio River System, United States
These rivers are infamous for their floods, but their floodplains mean rich, fertile soil for farmers. In April 1927, heavy rains began to fall in the Mississippi Valley. By June, flooding increased until nearly 26,000 square miles (67,340 sq km) lay under water.

② The Orinoco River, Venezuela
Indigenous peoples subsist on fish caught from this 1,300 mile (2,092 km) river. They live in houses on stilts to protect them from floods. But in 1999, rains caused floods and mud slides, destroying homes and killing more than 20,000 people.

③ The Amazon River System, South America
This system dumps 58 billion gallons (219 billion liters) of water into the ocean *every second*. In 1998 during a full moon, ocean tides pushed a 16-foot- (5-m-) high wall of water more than 400 miles (644 km) inland. Few villages have been built along the Amazon's banks, because the river floods about twice each year.

④ The Nile River, Egypt
In ancient Egypt, farmers depended on the annual flooding of the Nile to enrich the soil. Today, farmers count on heavy irrigation and flooding to produce their rice crops. Without this yearly flooding event, Egypt would not have had enough food to support what became one of the world's great civilizations.

⑤ The Niger River, Nigeria
In 1998, this river caused its worst flooding in thirty years. When officials saw the Kainji Dam about to collapse, they opened its floodgates, and more than three hundred thousand homes and farms were destroyed.

⑥ The Tana River, Kenya
Kenya's longest river flows through a semiarid region and then into a wide valley, where the soil is rich and fertile. But nature can upset the balance: In the fall of 1997, East Africa had ten times its normal rainfall, after months of severe drought. By November, the Tana had burst its banks in hundreds of places.

ASIA

EUROPE

The Yellow River
(Huang Ho)
8

CHINA

The Nile River
4

EGYPT

AFRICA

The Ganges River
7

The Yangtze River
9

5 The Niger River

NIGERIA

BANGLADESH

6 The Tana River

KENYA

Yangtze River in China

AUSTRALIA

7 **The Ganges River, Bangladesh**
Most land here is just above sea level on a delta formed by three huge rivers. Farmers depend on seasonal monsoons for raising crops of rice, wheat, jute, and tea. Torrential rains in 1998 left three-quarters of the country underwater for two months. The flood was the worst in Bangladesh in 100 years.

8 **The Yellow River (Huang Ho), China**
This river is one of the world's muddiest, carrying about 2 pounds (.9 kilograms) of silt for every cubic foot (.03 cubic m) of water. Although enriching the soil of the surrounding farmland for centuries,

the Yellow River's flooding has also struck with such devastating consequences that the river is called "China's Sorrow."

9 **The Yangtze River, China**
When dikes gave way in 1931, a flood killed 140,000 people and washed away much of the fertile soil. In 1954, floods claimed another 30,000 lives and forced officials to start building the Three Gorges Dam in 1994. Most of China's 1.2 billion people still live in floodplains.

Activity

ONCE IN 100 YEARS Floods happen in cycles; many rivers flood every year; some flood twice each year. But some kinds of floods, called "100-year-floods," happen on average only once in a century. Use the Internet to learn about one of these floods. Find out what caused it, the amount of land it covered, and other interesting information. Then write a report that includes a map of the river, with shading to indicate the river's floodplain.

Soaked

Johnstown, Pennsylvania, May 31, 1889, 3:10 P.M.

It had been raining heavily for several days, and the water in nearby rivers was rising dangerously. While flooding was nothing new in this town (left) in western Pennsylvania where the Little Conemaugh River crosses the Stonycreek River, this year the spring rains had been worse than usual. On the night of Thursday, May 30, the rain fell.

By Friday afternoon, the dam on the South Fork reservoir in the mountains 14 miles (23 km) northeast of Johnstown could no longer hold the water. Suddenly it collapsed, sending a wall of water 23 feet (7 m) high rushing toward an unsuspecting and unprepared town. Thousands died in the disaster, the worst flood in U.S. history.

A nineteenth-century lithograph of the Johnstown flood

Geography Is Destiny

Disaster struck Johnstown because of its physical surroundings. The waters of the South Fork reservoir, also known as Conemaugh Lake, feed South Fork Run. This river flows into the Little Conemaugh River and runs down a valley to mix with the Stonycreek River 14 miles (23 km) below, in Johnstown.

A Room with a View

Wreckage from the flood

On June 1, 1889, George C. Gibbs, assistant editor of the *Johnstown Tribune*, reported what he saw from the newspaper's second-floor office.

> *As we write at noon, Johnstown is again under water and all about us the tide is rising. Wagons have for hours been passing along the streets, carrying people from submerged points to places of safety, and boats, floating as jauntily as upon the bosom of a river, have traversed the thoroughfares in the lower part of town, removing pent-up inmates from homes to which partial ruin has come thrice within as many years.*

Seen from Johnstown Hill

An article in the *New York Sun* includes an eyewitness account from Johnstown Hill.

> *The deserted street became black with people running for their lives. An instant later the flood came and licked them up with one surging and whirling mass of water, which swept away house after house with a rapidity that even the eye could not follow.*

Just outside of town, passengers evacuated the cars of a Pennsylvania Railroad train bound for New York. People scrambled for the safety of a nearby hill just as a wall of water washed out the tracks. Still, thirty-seven passengers and crew members were killed.

Up on the Roof

Victor Heiser, who had just moved his family's horses to safety on higher ground, wrote about the moment the floodwaters struck his home when he was sixteen.

> *My ears were stunned by the most terrifying noise I had ever heard in my sixteen years of life. The dreadful roar was punctuated with a succession of tremendous crashes.*

His father, who was at a second-floor window of their house, signalled wildly for Victor to climb onto the roof of the barn rather than trying to get back to the house.

> *From my perch I could see a huge wall advancing with incredible rapidity down the diagonal street. . . . As this wall struck Washington Street broadside, my boyhood home was crushed like an eggshell before my eyes, and I saw it disappear.*

As the barn was swept away by the floodwaters, Victor clung desperately to its roof. Finally he managed to leap onto the roof of a house.

> *For years thereafter I was visited by recurring dreams in which I have lived over and over again the fearful experience of hanging with my fingernails dug deep into the water-softened shingles, knowing in the end that I must let go. . . . It was not yet 4:30. Three thousand had been wiped out in less than ten minutes.*

Looking Forward

Johnstown has been hit by floods twice since the Great Flood, in 1936 and again in 1977, but neither was as devastating as the 1889 flood. Each time, the town repaired the damage and reinforced the dam. History has taught the citizens of Johnstown how to be prepared.

Activity

WATER PLUGS How much do you know about dams? Did you know that there are about 800,000 small dams, 40,000 large dams, and more than 300 major dams in the world? Most are made of one of three kinds of material—concrete, masonry, or earth. Use the Internet to research dams made of each of these building materials. Then create a chart that compares examples of each dam type. Include on your chart information such as: kind of dam (e.g., concrete gravity, concrete arch); main purpose of dam (e.g., hydroelectric power, reservoir, recreation); name of river dammed; location (state or country); height; and width. Also include a picture of each dam on the chart.

DIGGIN' UP THE

Soil is constantly being created and destroyed. But on average, the soil on Earth's surface is only 6 inches (15 cm) deep. In the past 500 years, Earth has gained approximately 1 inch (2.5 cm) of new soil. Here's how:

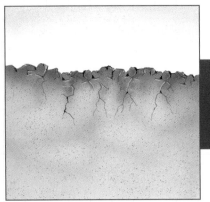

Bedrock on Earth's surface began to crack from assaults by rain, ice, freezing, and thawing.

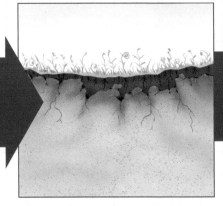

Lichen grew on the cracked rock. The acids secreted by these plants caused the rock to crumble slowly over many years.

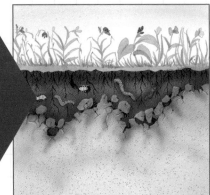

Horizons, or layers of soil began to form. The topsoil, or the A horizon, includes organic matter from decayed plants and animals. Just below is the B horizon, which contains minerals washed down from the topsoil. The C horizon below that is the original parent material. Bedrock lies at the bottom.

What's It Made Of?

Most soil comes from the rock that was broken down by weathering and chemical processes over thousands of years. This diagram shows the components of an average soil sample.

Scientists who study soil are called pedologists.

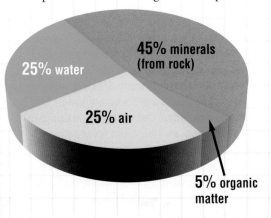

45% minerals (from rock)

25% water

25% air

5% organic matter

Weather's Role

Climate has a lot to do with making soil. It affects how quickly wind and water break down rock, and how much organic material is added to the soil

Places with warm temperatures and high humidity produce rich organic soil most easily because they encourage plant and animal growth as well as decay. Farmers and greenhouses prefer humus, or soil full of organic material, because it has lots of nutrients for plants and holds water well.

Desert regions with little precipitation have small amounts of organic matter in their soil, which means many plants don't thrive. Often sandy desert soils do not hold much water.

Salt of the Earth

We'd be nowhere without soil. We need it to grow crops necessary for our survival. But not all soil is the same, and how much we can cultivate in a particular area depends on the type of soil found there. Agriculture is the result of the surrounding landscape, which in turn is linked to the kind of soil you'll find in any given place.

The texture of soil depends on the size of its individual particles. Let's take a closer look at the three types: sand, silt, and clay.

Sand Many minerals can be found in sandy soil, which has the largest particles. The soil in arid regions tends to be sandy, which explains why Arizona and New Mexico aren't good areas for raising crops. But sand has other uses. Over time we've used it to make glass and various works of art.

Native Americans made this jar from clay.

In Tibet, Buddhist monks use colored sand to create paintings that take days or weeks to complete. When finished, they sweep up the sand and pour it into a river or stream, to show that nothing lasts forever.

Clay The soil with the finest particles (so small that they can only be seen with a microscope) is clay. Clay will hold water much better than sandy soil, but water still doesn't flow easily through it. As a result, soil with a large percentage of clay is not good for cultivating crops. Yet clay is an essential material to us: Native Americans have used clay for thousands of years to make everything from bowls to adobe houses.

Silt Soil rich in silt has much smaller particles than sand. It lies in the floodplains of major rivers. Silt has created rich farmland in some midwestern states along the Missouri and Mississippi Rivers. People have lived in floodplains over the centuries to take advantage of the rich soil for raising crops. Animals have adapted to take advantage of the rich mud found near rivers and lakes, too. Elephants, for example, take mud baths to keep their skin cool and safe from sunburn.

An elephant takes a mud bath.

Water Drop

You are a molecule of water floating along in the Pacific Ocean with a quadrillion or so of your closest water-molecule friends. You've all been on Earth a long, long time—since before the dinosaurs . . . even before the first plants. Today, you and your friends have been bobbing near the ocean's surface. The Sun is beaming down and you're beginning to feel its energy transform you. You feel speeded up. Suddenly, you're no longer part of a liquid. And you're no longer in the ocean. You're a gas!

Life's a Gas

Up, up you go, rising like a balloon . . . higher and higher. It's a giddy feeling, but it doesn't last and you're getting cold. You need to reconnect with a few of your old molecule friends, and you find just the spot: a nice speck of dust. A bunch of you latch onto the dust and condense into tiny water droplets. You look around. There are billions more like your group, and together you have formed a rather impressive looking cloud. Then a wind comes up and blows you all northeast.

You hope to get back to the ocean before too long. After all, 97 percent of all the water on Earth hangs out there. But no such luck. You drift over land, and much of it is covered with ice. When a million or so of you get together, you're no longer lighter than air. The tug of gravity takes over. You fall, but slowly, as part of a snowflake.

Cold Landing

Wouldn't you know it! You land smack dab in the middle of a snow-covered mountain. More flakes pile on top of you. No choice but to relax and go with the icy flow. Time passes. Lots of it.

But then you start to feel the Sun again. Suddenly, you realize you've melted into flowing water! You have forgotten how much fun it is to slide down hills. You puddle into a pool and rest awhile until a huge hairy animal with big, curved tusks sucks you up into its snout. Twenty minutes later, you come out another end.

Goin' Down

This time, you sink deep into the ground and nestle between chunks of soil and rock. You're in a huge underground reservoir called an aquifer. You know you're in for a long wait, but water molecules are patient, after all. Maybe a plant will absorb you into its roots, and you'll pass into the air again.

Ten thousand or so years pass.

One day, a big tube made of something you've never seen before drops into your quiet reservoir. You're sucked up into it and carried a long distance. Eventually, you leave the darkness and pour forth into a clear container of some kind. A strange, nearly hairless animal raises the container to its mouth, sloshes you around a bit, and spits you into a basin. Gravity pulls you down into another dark tube. What next?

Riding the Rapids

After a long dark ride, you follow gravity into a major river. You are homesick for that great big ocean. "What's the name of this river?" you ask your water-molecule mates. "The Rio Grande," one of them says. You shake your hydrogen bond, wondering what language that poor molecule was speaking.

You go with the flow for days and days. As you pick up more water mates, you also collect an assortment of weird chemicals. Not just salts and minerals and a bit of animal waste like before, but unfamiliar molecules that you can't break apart very easily. You detour through a few fish innards, but the fish become few and far between when the strange chemicals are strongest. Eventually, though, you begin to bump into old sea salts and you know your journey is nearly complete.

Full Circle

When you swoop into a shark's mouth as it clamps down on a fish, you realize you're really home. Those sharks have been around a long time. Gravity has led you back to Mother Ocean—this time, the Gulf of Mexico. You love being a part of this wonderful water world. And you take pride in knowing that without you—without water in all phases— the planet just wouldn't be the same. Life simply couldn't thrive in all its strange and wonderful forms.

But enough philosophy. You're free to splash around again as you please. It's time to just hang out for a few millennia and *flow* with the currents. One day you'll hop on the water cycle again, but for now, the Sun's out of sight and you just don't have the energy.

Activity

CYCLE IN A BOWL To see up close how the water cycle works, add enough water to cover the bottom of a glass bowl. Cover the top of the bowl with plastic wrap. On top of the wrap, place an ice cube that has been wrapped in plastic or put in a sealable plastic bag. Set the bowl in a sunny window. Write a note about what you think will happen inside the bowl. Check your experiment after half an hour. Where did the water that collects on the underside of the plastic wrap covering the bowl come from? Write an explanation of what happened.

Seeking THE SOURCE

If you're a hydrologist, you may look at Earth as one big liquid lab. Hydrologists study water, which covers 71 percent of the planet. But would you expect to find yourself working in a desert?

Absolutely!

"Water can be studied virtually anywhere on Earth," says Karl Pohlmann, a hydrologist at the Desert Research Institute in Nevada. "But it is especially interesting where it is rare. In the Earth's deserts, for example."

Pohlmann and his colleagues from the institute explored a region where the Mojave, Sonora, and Great Basin deserts converge. The National Park Service was concerned about rapid population growth in southern Nevada, particularly the Las Vegas Valley, and how it might affect water resources near the Lake Mead National Recreation Area. Although the area looks dry and barren, it has more than eighty springs and seeps, water found on the surface that flows from an underground source. Pohlmann's challenge: to find the source of the underground water.

GOING UNDERGROUND

As elsewhere on Earth, water in the desert lies in aquifers, or underground areas made of porous rock containing water. The water seeps through the rock through cracks and spaces between rock particles. Aquifers carry the water to springs and seeps.

But what refills the aquifers, and where does that water come from? Scientists had believed that rainwater was not a significant source, because high temperatures and low humidity would evaporate most of it. Pohlmann and his colleagues went to the springs to try to find some answers. Their method was to examine the condition of the water that seeped to the surface with a variety of tests and techniques.

WATER TESTS

They used a pH analyzer to help assess the condition of the aquifers. Then they took the water's temperature with a special probe. Finally, they used an electrical conductivity device to figure out the amount of dissolved minerals in the water. When the tests were complete, they put the information together to develop a profile of each seep or spring.

The next step in solving the

Hydrologist Karl Pohlmann studies the soil in the desert of Nevada to learn more about underground water sources.

mystery of where the water came from was to send samples to a lab, where scientists put the water through an even more specialized round of testing. They were looking for something specific: chemical components that would show the water had been exposed to certain processes in the atmosphere. "For example, these components would be different in rain falling at higher elevations than rain falling at lower elevations," explains Pohlmann.

Like other scientists, Pohlmann believed his findings would confirm that the water in many of the desert springs came from higher elevations, farther away. In fact, the testing showed that most or all of the water from the aquifers came from local rainfall at lower elevations. And that rainfall wasn't recent. Pohlmann found that water from even the smallest springs was not from recent rainfall, but had been replenished over several decades.

What does this mean? First of all, because rain falls so infrequently in the desert, the aquifers don't refill often. Also, the water in these aquifers has been there for some time. So anyone digging a well and tapping the water in those aquifers would be depleting a water source that took years to fill. And if lots of people started digging wells to supply new homes with water, the aquifers could come up empty for years and years.

"These small springs represent a delicate balance," Pohlmann concludes. "They would be

Desert plants flourish at a spring near Pohlmann's lab.

particularly sensitive to environmental changes, be they climactic or man-made."

THE DESERT AND BEYOND

Karl Pohlmann's discoveries will help the National Park Service better understand how to maintain the natural beauty and delicate ecosystem of the area. "The amount of water from these small springs may not be great," he explains, "but it is often the only source of water for a number of small, diverse plant and animal habitats that add a lot to the recreation area."

On a planet that is two-thirds water, it would seem that finding freshwater should be a snap. But most of the water above ground is saltwater in the oceans and seas. Hydrologists are working to find new sources of freshwater. According to the National Ground Water Association, the United States gets more than 700 billion gallons (2,649 billion l) of freshwater from the ground every day! Part of a hydrologist's job is to know where clean freshwater exists so people can drill wells.

And to Karl Pohlmann, that's just the beginning. "I find the study of water exciting," he says, "because water is a critical factor in so many aspects of our environment, from being a major component of all living things to having a major influence on the landscape around us."

Activity

EVAPORATION EXPLORATION After the next rainstorm, find a large mud puddle somewhere you can easily pass by each day. Write down all the information you can about it, including its location, size, shape, and depth of water. Now observe it every day for a week. Make careful notes each time about the changes you notice. At the end of the week, see if you can explain each change.

Earth's CELLAR

I magine a place underground as tall as a twenty-five-story building and one-third of a mile wide (.5 km) . . . a place filled with spires and columns that glisten as if they are covered by the drippings of hot candle wax. This vision is what greets visitors at the Great Room at New Mexico's Carlsbad Caverns, a monster cave that wanders underground for more than 23 dark miles (37 km).

How Water Digs a Cave

Millions of years ago, Carlsbad's limestone was a large underwater reef. After the sea drained away, movements in Earth's crust pushed the limestone upward. Soon the limestone was covered by soil and plants. This process caused fractures in the rock that gave water a chance to begin its work. When the water picked up carbon dioxide from the air (and became "carbonated" like soft drinks), it turned into a weak acid. As it flowed into cracks in the limestone, the soft rock began to dissolve. Slowly, existing spaces deepened into "black holes."

As the surface water migrated underground, the holes in the rock enlarged. Over time, gravity continued to force water downward through existing cracks, where it eroded through rock. Eventually, underground river systems formed, complete with lakes and waterfalls.

Stack 'em Up

The artistry of cave formation really begins when large chambers form and water uses a "drip brush" technique to make speleothems, or cave deposits. Stalagmites, stalactites, soda straws, drapery, cave pearls, popcorn, and other formations are

Sonora Caverns, Texas

the result of the minerals precipitating out of slowly dripping water. Here's how it works: Water becomes saturated with calcium carbonate when it dissolves limestone. It picks up carbon dioxide from the air. If the carbon dioxide concentration in the water is greater than the amount in the cave air, some of it will "fizz out" of the solution, like soda fizzing out of a freshly opened soft drink. When this happens, the water can't hold as much calcium carbonate, so it leaves some behind. What's left behind are icicle-like formations, which are called stalactites if they hang from the cave's ceiling and stalagmites if they rise from the cave floor.

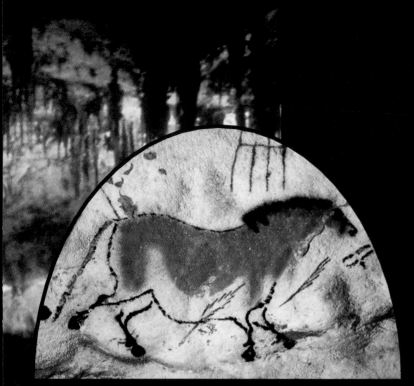

"Second Chinese Horse," Lascaux Cave, France

Cave Trivia

▶ The deepest known cave in the world, the Jean Bernard Cave in France, is nearly 1 mile (1.6 km) deep.

▶ Mammoth-Flint Ridge in Kentucky is the longest cave system ever explored. It has more than 190 miles (306 km) of interconnected passages and chambers.

▶ The Glowworm Cave in Waitomo, New Zealand, gets its name from fluorescent fly larvae that live on the ceilings of the cave and trap insects in sticky webs. They look like stars to people who take boats through the cave.

▶ The Carlsbad Caverns were discovered in 1901 when bats were seen pouring from cave openings, as they still do today.

DID YOU KNOW?
A cave scientist (above) is called a *speleologist*, and someone who explores and maps caves as a hobby is called a *spelunker*.

Caves in Danger

Although cave art dates back thousands of years, it can be destroyed in a matter of years, months, or even minutes. As caves attract more and more visitors, other problems result.

▶ The Lascaux Cave in France has paintings made by humans twenty thousand years ago. These attracted tourists, so air conditioning and lights were installed in the caves. Such additions altered the environment, which led to the deterioration of the art. To preserve the drawings, the caves were closed.

▶ In eastern Missouri, the flow of water into a cave changed when vegetation was cleared from its entrance. The water passed over the tracks of an Ice Age jaguar, partially covering them with sediment and hiding them from view.

▶ Creating new openings to caves has damaged them. This allows wind inside, bringing more moisture and freezing temperatures in winter, which quickly erodes cave formations.

Activity

LIMESTONE MELTDOWN To observe the effects of acid on limestone, put a piece of chalk (which is pure limestone) in a glass. Pour enough carbonated water into the glass to cover the chalk. Watch what happens. Record your observations every five minutes. Test the carbonated water on a few rocks outside. Can you tell which ones contain limestone? From your observations, do you think the area where you live is likely to have caves?

Trouble at RED ROCK RANCH

As Sheriff Clay Banks drove through the gate of the Red Rock Ranch, he could see a cloud of dry red dust billowing up behind the jeep in the rearview mirror. Down the road, Rock Fielding waited patiently for his arrival at the ranch house.

"Thanks for coming out so early," Rock Fielding said, offering the sheriff a freshly brewed cup of coffee.

"Not a problem, Rock. I'm normally up at the crack of dawn anyway," smiled Clay Banks. "So what's this about your prize stallion being rustled away in the night?"

"I don't think it happened more than two or three hours ago. I heard the dogs barking at about 3 A.M., and I thought it was just coyotes. But when I got up this morning, Valiant was gone."

"Mind if we take a look at the stables?" asked Sheriff Banks.

"Sure thing, Clay," Rock obliged. "They're near the stream out back."

"Any idea who might be interested in that horse?" asked the sheriff.

"Well, as a matter of fact, just last week I turned down three offers to sell him. Frankly, Valiant is worth a lot more than the offers I got."

"Looks like we've got something here," Sheriff Banks said suddenly, pointing to some footprints near the stables. He measured the length and width of each print. Then he scooped up a soil sample and sealed it in a plastic bag. "The dirt back here looks a lot richer than out front," the sheriff remarked, noticing a few blades of grass mixed in with the soil.

"Yes," Rock said proudly. "Horse manure makes great fertilizer for my little vegetable plot. I try to mix the manure with the dirt that's close to the stream. It's not great, but it's better than the other dry rocky stuff around here."

"Tell me, who made bids on Valiant? I'd like to go pay them a visit."

Thirty minutes later, Sheriff Banks knocked on Pete Moss's door at the

Pete Moss: Sample 2

Red Rock Ranch: Sample 1

Dusty Grimes: Sample 3

Lazy S Ranch and explained the situation.

"Well, Valiant's a nice horse, but I didn't go and steal him!" said Pete.

The sheriff noticed Pete's boots airing out by the door. They looked about the size of the footprints at Red Rock Ranch. "What have you been up to this morning?" he questioned.

"Digging out back. I'd like to have a pond by the end of summer. The ground is hard as rock out there. I have to soften it up with water before I can dig."

"I see," said Sheriff Banks. "Well, you don't mind if I do a little test on this mud on your boots, do ya?" He scraped a dirt sample into another bag and sealed it. "Thanks for your time, Pete," he said, tipping his hat. "I'll be on my way now."

A little later, the sheriff was face to face with Dusty Grimes near the corral of his Crooked River Ranch, questioning him about his morning's activities.

"You've got the wrong man, Sheriff," said Dusty, chewing on a toothpick. "I've just been unloading hay all morning. Was here all day yesterday, too."

"Well, if it's no trouble, I need to check your boots. We found some footprints at Fielding's ranch," explained Sheriff Banks. "It's just a routine matter."

"All right," Dusty laughed as he took off a boot. Its bottom had a thin layer of fine, sandy soil on it, which the sheriff scraped off into another plastic bag. He also worked off some of the caked dirt from the inside of the boot heel.

"Much appreciated, Dusty," smiled the sheriff as he left to see his next suspect.

"Howdy, Clay," waved Sandy Hill to the sheriff as he pulled up to the Flying H Ranch. "I heard there's some trouble."

"Yup, there's trouble all right. What's your alibi, Sandy?"

"I've been busy packing up my truck and horse trailer. I made a deal with a rancher in Dry Creek for one of his horses. But it's a six-hour drive, so I need to get a move on."

"Before you go, Sandy," the sheriff said, "I need to make sure you weren't at the crime scene." He explained the footprints and convinced Sandy to donate a dirt sample from her boots.

At noon, Rock Fielding's phone rang. "Hello?"

"Clay, here. I've just done some tests on these soil samples. I know who took Valiant."

What did the sheriff tell Rock?

Sandy Hill: Sample 4

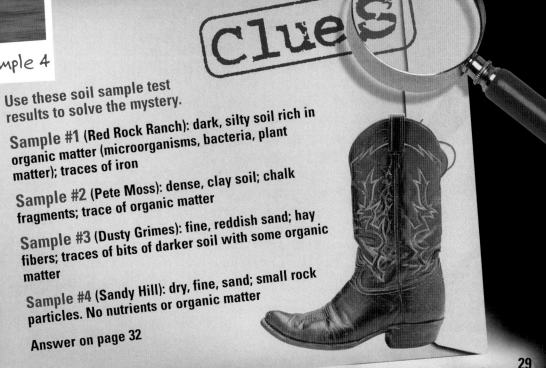

Use these soil sample test results to solve the mystery.

Sample #1 (Red Rock Ranch): dark, silty soil rich in organic matter (microorganisms, bacteria, plant matter); traces of iron

Sample #2 (Pete Moss): dense, clay soil; chalk fragments; trace of organic matter

Sample #3 (Dusty Grimes): fine, reddish sand; hay fibers; traces of bits of darker soil with some organic matter

Sample #4 (Sandy Hill): dry, fine, sand; small rock particles. No nutrients or organic matter

Answer on page 32

WATERLOGGED

Pool Table?

If plant roots don't absorb it, water sinks through cracks in the soil, sand, or rock until it stops at a layer of rock. It then fills the empty spaces above that layer. The top level of this underground water is called the water table. Water that seeps into this reservoir refills water that has been taken out by pumping or because it has flowed into aboveground streams and lakes.

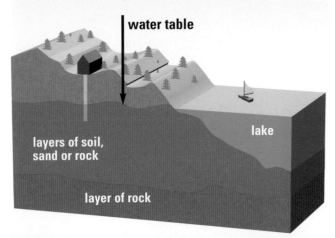

water table

lake

layers of soil, sand or rock

layer of rock

Water Counts!

On Earth, there are 326 million cubic miles (1.4 billion km³) of water! That's a lotta H_2O!

- 71 percent of Earth's surface is covered with water.
- Less than 1 percent of Earth's water is fresh.
- 96 percent of fresh-water is underground, or groundwater.
- 63 percent of ground-water pumped in the United States irrigates crops.
- 19 percent of groundwater goes into the public water supply in the United States, but 51 percent of our drinking water comes from the ground.
- About 492 billion gallons (18.7 trillion l) of ground-water in the United States are discharged into surface bodies of water every day. That's especially good to know during droughts.

99% saltwater

Living the Cool Life

Lake Vostok lies 12,000 feet (3,658 m) beneath Antarctica. Experts believe the water in the lake is one-half million to one million years old. Scientists are developing robots to explore the lake's depths. But in the meantime, researchers are examining samples from as deep as 4,000 feet (1,219 m) below the surface ice and finding microorganisms in the ice. Scientists have named them Klingon, Porpoise, and Mickey Mouse based on their shapes

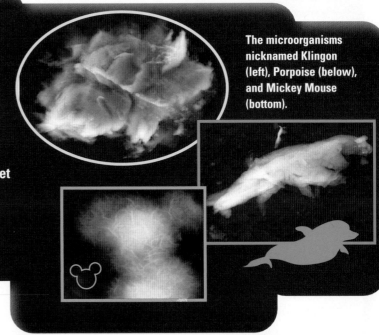

The microorganisms nicknamed Klingon (left), Porpoise (below), and Mickey Mouse (bottom).

Well, Well...

Some wells can pump water directly out of the ground. They are called artesian wells, after the Artois region of France, where such wells were first dug in the twelfth century. The water is under pressure because it is sandwiched between layers of clay or rock. If the pressure is great enough, the water just spurts out when the well is dug.

A house in a sinkhole.

Sinking Feelings

- The San Joaquin Valley in California is sinking. Why? People drained huge amounts of water from the ground for agriculture. Some wells in this valley remove as much as 3,200 gallons (12,109 l) of water every minute. The rocks that held the water then collapsed.

- How would you feel if your house suddenly fell into a hole? That's happened in Florida and Texas, where the land is composed of limestone, salt beds, and other kinds of rock that are dissolved by flowing water. So empty spaces and caverns develop underground. The land stays intact until the hole gets too big, then it simply collapses . . . taking whatever was on top along with it!

River Characters

Read the clues below to name the rivers.

Favorite cowboy river.
[Rio Grande or Red River]

Gandhi's sacred river.
[Ganges]

Huckleberry Finn rafted down it.
[Mississippi]

Cleopatra floated down it on a barge.
[Nile]

Washington threw a silver dollar across it.
[Potomac]

Queen Elizabeth's river.
[Thames]

Johann Strauss composed a waltz about this one.
[Danube]

TUG OF WAR, ANYONE?

Le Claire   Port Byron

Port Byron, Illinois, and Le Claire, Iowa, have a special connection to the Mississippi. Every August, the towns hold the Great River Tugfest. Teams assemble on either side of the river, holding opposite ends of a 2,400-foot (732-m) rope. Members of the losing team usually fall in and get a sweet taste of river mud!

Lifeline

Have you ever thought about the water that comes out of your tap? Where does it come from? It could come from a well, a lake, a river, or a reservoir.

Is it always safe to drink? Perhaps it is tested from time to time. Perhaps chemicals are added, or the water is treated in a special way so that it remains drinkable. Most likely you have a water treatment plant near where you live, where trained personnel are doing this work.

Imagine your world without faucets and plumbing and, most of all, clean, easily accessible water—a world where YOU have to find pure water for drinking and cooking on your own.

Another issue is soil—perhaps there are people in your community who are responsible for looking after the soil in your neck of the woods. You know what can happen when land is cleared of its plant life—EROSION. Or you might be near mountains where water might have a chance to make a speedy slide toward your home.

1. Divide into two teams: Water and Land.

2. First order of business for both teams: Find out where to get information on conservation in your community. Is there a local water resources board? Soil conservation organizations?

3. Water Team: Find out as much as you can about your water supply—where it comes from, its quality, problems with contamination at the source or along

delivery routes, and so on. Don't forget to look at water history in your community. Did your town always get its water from the same source? Has drought ever been a major problem? What emergency procedures are in place to deal with water shortages?

4. Land Team: Find out as much as you can about soil conservation in your area. Are there any major problems with erosion? Are they being fixed? Might the erosion lead to floods or dust storms? Has the land in your area been overgrazed or worn out by poor farming practices? Are there problems with sinkholes or land subsidence? Are there major soil conservation projects underway in your area? What's missing in local conservation efforts?

5. As you assemble your data, create a large wall map of the community. Show reservoirs, lakes, wells, and water treatment facilities, as well as soil and water conservation projects such as dams, erosion control initiatives, and so on. Write particular problems you've pinpointed, such as "Badly eroded land . . . danger of severe water runoff" or "Petroleum contamination of groundwater," on small cards and pin at appropriate points on the map. Also highlight any soil and water conservation initiatives that are being planned or are underway.

6. Have a class discussion about how you can get involved in community conservation efforts.

ANSWER Solve-It-Yourself Mystery, pages 28–29:

Dusty Grimes stole the horse. Bits of dirt from the soles of his boot matched the soil at the scene of the crime. Sheriff Banks noticed that the footprint happened to be in topsoil that was rich in nutrients. This was evident because of the grass growing in the ground, and because Rock admitted he was introducing fertilizer into the soil. So the sheriff knew the culprit would have evidence of the top layer of soil on his or her boot.

Most of the land around the ranch is dry, rocky, and sandy, with little vegetation. Erosion has worn away most of the top layer, exposing the next layer of soil. Such soil is heavy in mineral deposits, like iron, which give a reddish color to the dirt. This was the kind of soil in the driveway of the Red Rock Ranch and on Sandy Hill's boot.

The soil on Pete Moss's boot had evidence of soil from a much deeper layer of subsoil. This soil has large deposits of chalk, is extremely compact and rocky, and has almost no organic matter in it. The dirt on Pete's boot was evidence that he had recently dug a very deep hole.

32